/ OFF TO THE RACES

Snocross

Thomas Kingsley Troupe

45th Parallel Press

Published in the United States of America by Cherry Lake Publishing Group
Ann Arbor, Michigan
www.cherrylakepublishing.com

Reading Adviser: Beth Walker Gambro, MS, Ed., Reading Consultant, Yorkville, IL

PHOTOS CREDITS:
©www.shutterstock.com, Cover ©AerialVision_it, page 2 ©Mark Bonham, page 4-5 ©Glen Gaffney| Dreamstime.com, page 6-7 ©Anton Parsukov, page 8 ©Boombardier (CCAS - https://creativecommons.org/licenses/by-sa/3.0/deed.en), Page 9 ©Yuri Kravchenko, page 10 ©Edgar Lee Espe, page 11© Glen Gaffney| Dreamstime.com, page 12-13 ©Konstantin Zaykov| Dreamstime.com, page 13 ©Crystal Wallem- www.crystalwallemphotography.com, page 14 © Christophe Moratal| Dreamstime.com, page 15 ©Crystal Wallem- www.crystalwallemphotography.com, page 16-17 ©Crystal Wallem- www.crystalwallemphotography.com, page 18-19 ©Crystal Wallem- www.crystalwallemphotography.com, page 21 ©Christophe Moratal| Dreamstime.com, page 22-23 © Christophe Moratal| Dreamstime.com, page 23 ©Sergey Borisenkol Dreamstime.com, ©Parilov, page 25 ©Artzzz| Dreamstime.com, page 26-27 ©Crystal Wallem- www.crystalwallemphotography.com, page 28-29 ©Crystal Wallem- www.crystalwallemphotography.com, page 31 ©Artzzz| Dreamstime.com

Produced for Cherry Lake Publishing by bluedooreducation.com

Copyright © 2026 by Cherry Lake Publishing Group

All rights reserved. No part of this book may be reproduced or utilized in any form or by any means without written permission from the publisher.

45th Parallel Press is an imprint of Cherry Lake Publishing Group.

Library of Congress Cataloging-in-Publication Data has been filed and is available at catalog.loc.gov.
Printed in the United States of America

Note from Publisher: Websites change regularly, and their future contents are outside of our control. Supervise children when conducting any recommended online searches for extended learning opportunities.

ABOUT THE AUTHOR
Thomas Kingsley Troupe is the author of over 300 books for young readers. When he's not writing, he enjoys reading, playing video games, and hunting ghosts as part of the Twin Cities Paranormal Society. Otherwise, he's probably taking a nap or something. TKT lives in Woodbury, MN, with his two sons.

Table of Contents

CHAPTER 1
Introduction 4

CHAPTER 2
Snocross History 8

CHAPTER 3
Snocross Events 14

CHAPTER 4
Snowmobiles & Gear 20

CHAPTER 5
Snocross Racers 26

Did You Know? 30
Find Out More 32
Glossary 32
Index 32

Chapter 1
Introduction

Snowmobiles rumble to life. The whine of the engines drowns out the crowd noise. All of the racers are at the starting line. They rev their machines. The racers are all waiting. The light turns green. They're off!

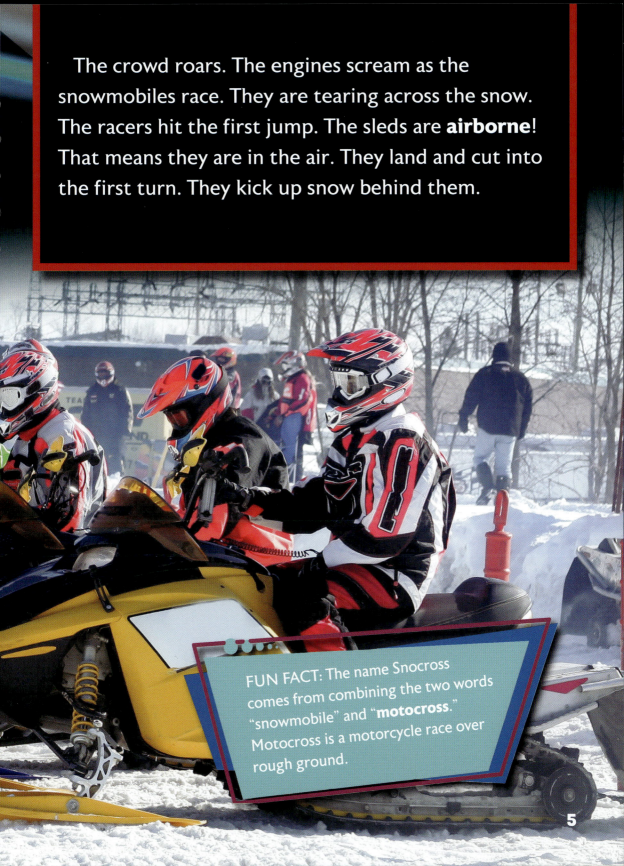

The crowd roars. The engines scream as the snowmobiles race. They are tearing across the snow. The racers hit the first jump. The sleds are **airborne**! That means they are in the air. They land and cut into the first turn. They kick up snow behind them.

FUN FACT: The name Snocross comes from combining the two words "snowmobile" and "**motocross**." Motocross is a motorcycle race over rough ground.

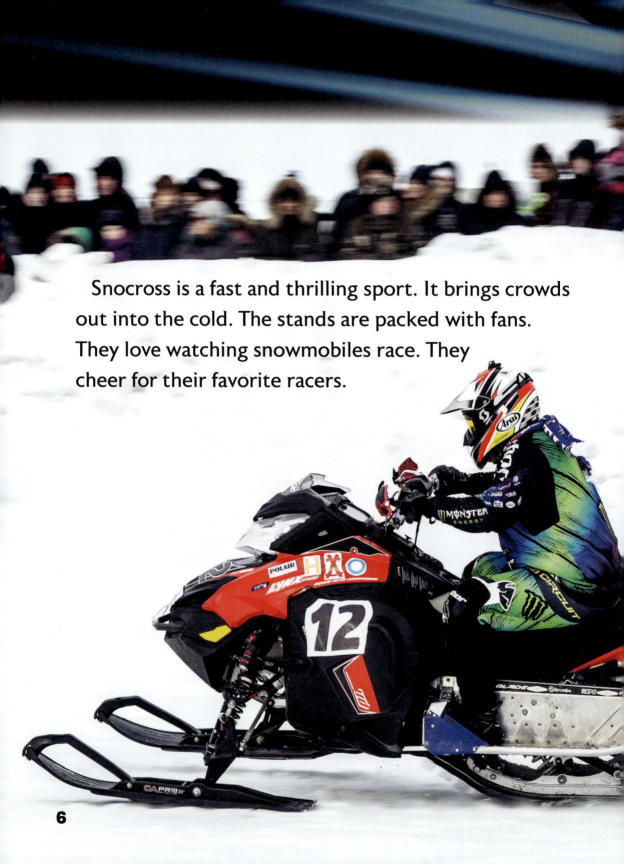

Snocross is a fast and thrilling sport. It brings crowds out into the cold. The stands are packed with fans. They love watching snowmobiles race. They cheer for their favorite racers.

Snocross racers love the thrill of the race. They plan how to pass other sleds. They try to move ahead. At each jump, they hold on tight. Snocross is awesome, but dangerous. Racers can flip off their snowmobiles. Their ride could land on them. They risk their lives with every race.

Snocross is not for people afraid of the cold. Is the action worth the risk? Let's learn more!

Chapter 2
Snocross History

Snocross is a fairly new sport. Joseph-Armand Bombardier invented the first snowmobile in 1935. It didn't look like snowmobiles today. It looked like a car sitting on skis and tank tracks. It could hold 2 to 3 passengers.

A rider uses an old snowmobile to travel across the snow.

Snowmobiles changed over time. They became smaller and easier to manufacture. Soon, many people had snowmobiles. They helped people travel in snowy conditions. For fun, riders raced each other. The snowy countryside became raceways.

Joseph Armand-Bombardier created a different snowmobile much earlier. In 1922, at age 15, he tested his new invention. He fixed up a Model T Ford car engine. He put the engine on 2 wooden sleds. The engine made a propeller spin. It moved fast enough to push the sleds.

The first official snowmobile race happened in 1962. The Beausejour Winter Festival was in Manitoba, Canada. Thousands of fans gathered. Six snowmobiles competed. They raced around a rough, snowy track. They reached speeds of 15 miles (25 kilometers) per hour.

1960s snowmobile

The tracks were flat and circular. It was like watching a car race. Large clusters of racers roared past the crowds. The noise was almost deafening. Snowmobiles were very loud back then. They disturbed nature. People wanted to ban snowmobiles.

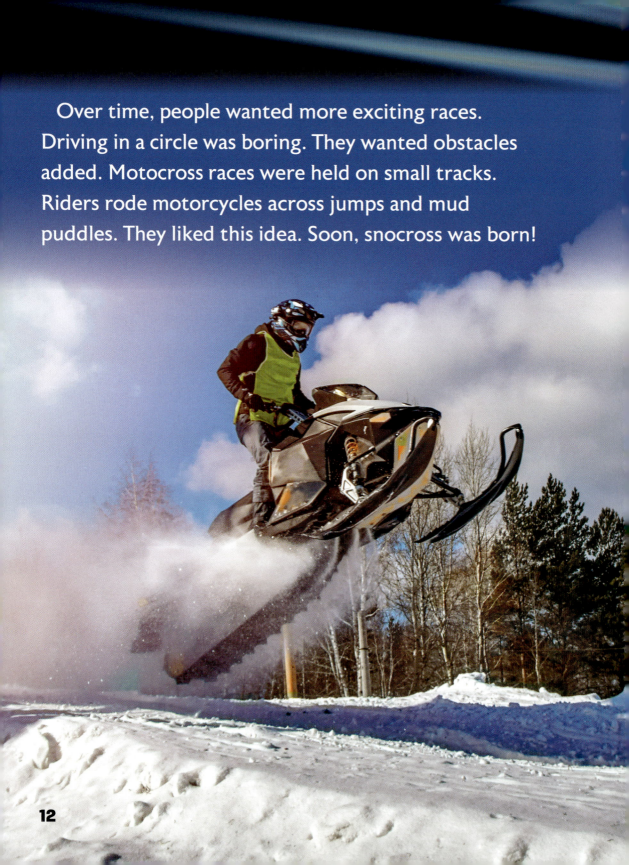

Over time, people wanted more exciting races. Driving in a circle was boring. They wanted obstacles added. Motocross races were held on small tracks. Riders rode motorcycles across jumps and mud puddles. They liked this idea. Soon, snocross was born!

Snocross was part of the X Games in 1998. The games were held in Crested Butte, Colorado. Around 25,000 people came to watch. The snowmobiles hit speeds close to 60 miles (96.6 km) per hour. The excitement caught on. Snocross was a hit!

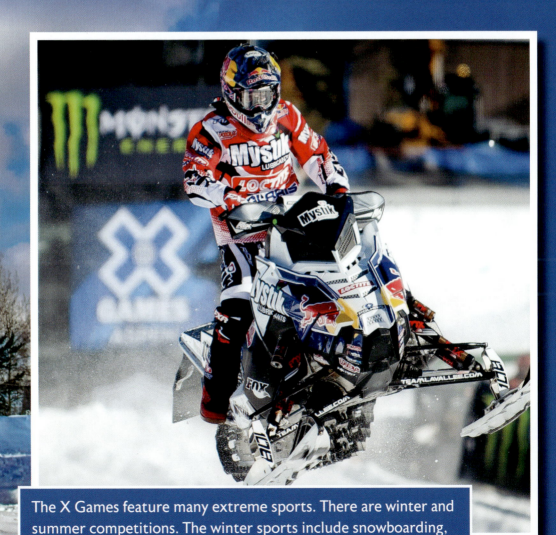

The X Games feature many extreme sports. There are winter and summer competitions. The winter sports include snowboarding, skiing, and snocross.

Chapter 3
Snocross Events

Snocross racers compete on a track. Sometimes they must compete in **qualifying** races. Qualifying means testing for skill. Riders have to earn their spots in the **lineup**, the positions they will take at the start of the race. The top racers from each qualifying race advance. The final race is where the best racers compete. Whoever wins the final race is the champion.

There are usually 8 racers per race. If there are too many, the track is crowded. The number of laps can vary. The race is fast and furious. Snow flies everywhere. Snowmobiles rush by at high speeds. Officials use flags to signal the racers. Flags let racers know if rules were broken or if there are crashes ahead.

Snocross jumps are called **moguls**. They are piles of hard snow on the race tracks. Moguls are also seen in downhill skiing. Snocross racers call moguls "bumps." These obstacles send snowmobiles flying high.

Snocross races have many sharp turns. This makes it difficult to get around the track. Snowmobiles are forced to slow down a little. Others can to try to pass. There are also bumps and jumps. It makes races exciting.

Snowmobiles have shocks that soften landings.

The biggest snocross event is held every year. It is called the AMSOIL Snocross National. Races are held in the United States and Canada. The first race was held in 1992 in Duluth, Minnesota, with 236 racers.

Snowmobile racers call leaving the ground "air-time."

The winners for all the events compete. They face off in the AMSOIL Snocross Championship. In 2024, 1,000 racers participated.

The competition groups racers in different classes. They are divided by age, engine speed, and skill level to give everyone a fair chance.

Chapter 4
Snowmobiles & Gear

Snocross snowmobiles must meet **specifications**. Specifications are detailed plans and guidelines. A fast snowmobile is needed to compete. Snowmobiles from the past were too heavy. They didn't move quick enough. Snocross snowmobiles are smaller and lighter. This makes them faster. It makes them better for tight corners.

Jumps in older snowmobiles were difficult. They weren't light enough to get big air. When they did jump, landing damaged them. Newer snowmobiles have special **suspension systems**. Suspension systems absorb the shock of hard landings. This helps the rider stay on the machine and stay safe. Snowmobiles are built for rough conditions. Keeping the sled together is important. A wrecked snowmobile can't finish a race.

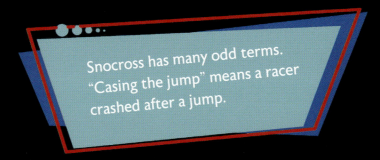

Snocross has many odd terms. "Casing the jump" means a racer crashed after a jump.

20

The track on a snowmobile is what pushes the sled around the course. Some racers will **modify** their track. Modify means change. Modifying changes how the track works. They can add studs to the bottom. The studs are little spiky bumps. They help the track grip the ice and snow. The course can get icy after many laps. The studs often make a difference.

The skis on a racing snowmobile are usually narrower than on most other snowmobiles. Narrow skis make it easier to **maneuver**, or turn, the machine. If the skis are too wide, the turns are wider. Sharp turns win races!

a snowmobile ski

snowmobile tracks

It's important for snocross riders to practice safety. They need to wear special gear. It helps protect them from harm.

Every racer wears a helmet. It protects the head. The helmet should have a visor on it. The visor shields the driver's eyes from snow, ice, and wind. Every racer also wears a padded vest. The vest protects the chest, back, and shoulders. A neck brace will help protect a racer's neck, spine, and collar bones.

Knee pads and shin pads are worn too. They help keep a racer's legs safe. Boots with good ankle support are required. Light gloves are worn to keep hands warm. The gloves have small pads on them. They are flexible enough to work snowmobile controls.

Chapter 5
Snocross Racers

Snocross can be a tough sport. It takes racers years of practice. They enter lots of races every season. They make changes to their sleds. Great snocross racers have quick reflexes. They have good **coordination**. This is the ability to move and react quickly. They are aware of other racers.

Teamwork is part of snocross. Racers should follow their crew's advice. The crew helps keep their snowmobile running smoothly.

Snocross is dangerous. Racers need to know the risks. They need to know their snowmobiles' limits. High speeds and big jumps can be tough. They need to ride smart and safe.

Professional snocross racers have support teams that include a mechanic.

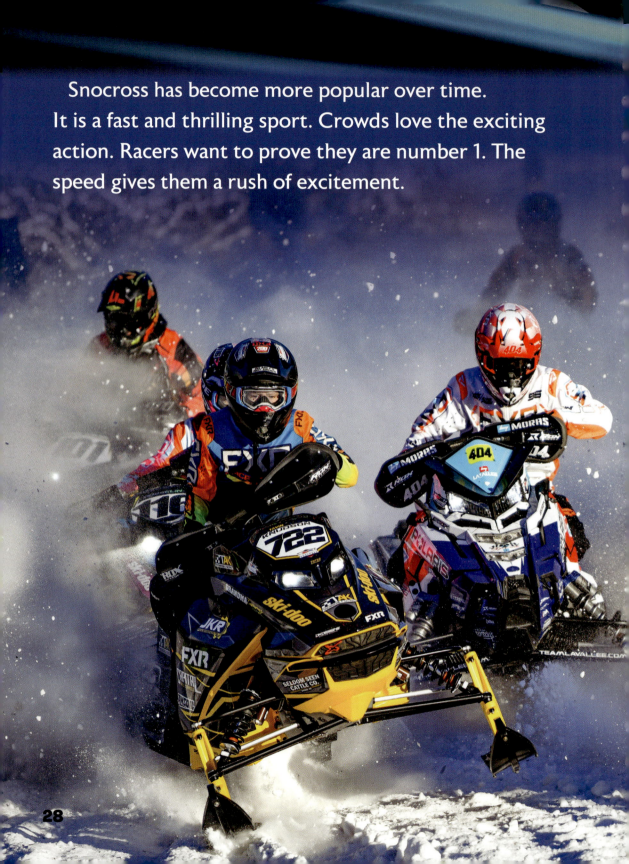

Snocross has become more popular over time. It is a fast and thrilling sport. Crowds love the exciting action. Racers want to prove they are number 1. The speed gives them a rush of excitement.

Snocross races will get better every year. New courses will be built. The snowmobiles will get better. The race to the finish will get faster. Want to see for yourself? Find out if there's a snocross event happening near you. Watch the sport for yourself. Off to the races!

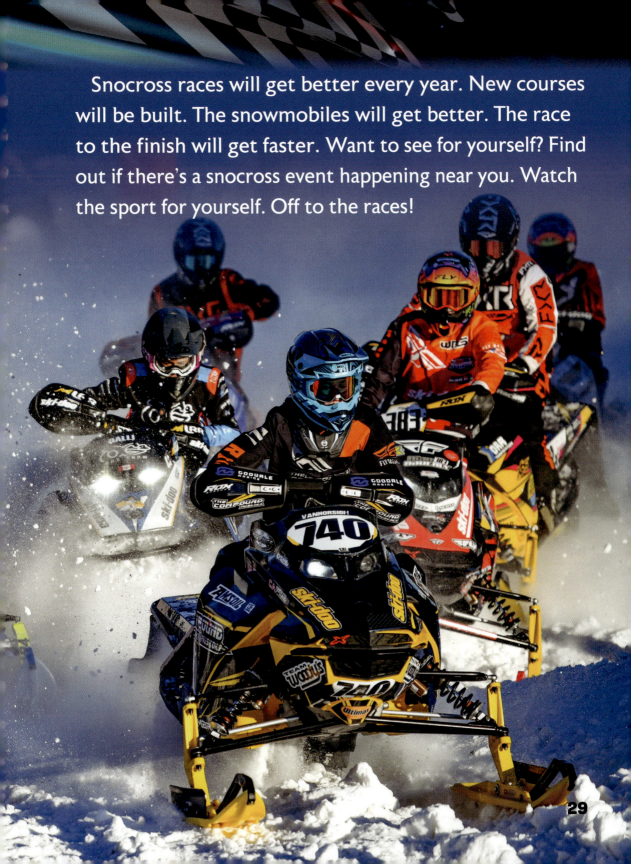

Did You Know?

handlebars and steering: used to steer and stop the machine

high-powered engine: gives the sled its speed, some engines are custom built

hood: covers the engine and protects it from the snow

shocks: allow the machine to jump and land softly

snow flap: helps keep snow from flying in other racers' faces

skis: steer and cut through the snow

track: pushes the sled through the snow

windshield: helps protect the driver from wind and cold air; many racers remove their windshields to make their sleds faster

Find Out More

BOOKS
Abdo, Kenny. *Snocross*. Minneapolis, MN: Abdo Publishing, 2018.

Bailer, Darice. *Snowmobile Snocross*. Minneapolis, MN: Lerner Publishing, 2014.

WEBSITES
Search these online sources with an adult:

Snocross | Kiddle

Snowmobiling | PBS

Glossary

airborne (EHR-born) being off the ground

coordination (koh-or-duh-NAY-shun) the ability to use different body parts to complete a task easily

lineup (LYEN-up) how the racers are positioned at the start of a race

maneuver (muh-NOO-vur) a movement or change in direction requiring skill

modify (MAH-duh-fye) to change something slightly to improve it

moguls (MOH-gulz) small piles of hard snow on a snocross track or ski slope

motocross (MOH-toh-krahs) a motorcycle race over a course of rough terrain

qualifying (KWAH-luh-fye-ing) meeting the requirements to be included in a race

specifications (speh-suh-fuh-KAY-shunz) a set of requirements or details to be followed

suspension systems (suh-SPEN-shun SIS-stuhms) series of springs and shock absorbers attached to wheels or skis

Index

AMSOIL Snocross National 18

Bombardier, Joseph-Armand 8, 9

competition(s) 4, 13, 19

engine(s) 4, 5, 9, 19, 30

jumps 12, 16, 17, 20, 27, 30

safety 24
skis 8, 23

tracks 8, 10–12, 14–17, 22

X Games 13